This Is Your Brain on the Internet

This Is Your Brain on the Internet

Michael Sunday

Ziff-Davis Press
Emeryville, California

Copy Editor	Nicole Clausing
Project Coordinator	Cort Day
Cover Design and Illustration	Regan Honda
Word Processing	Howard Blechman
Page Layout	Bruce Lundquist and M.D. Barrera
Illustration	Sarah Ishida and Mina Reimer

Ziff-Davis Press books are produced on a Macintosh computer system with the following applications: FrameMaker®, Microsoft® Word, QuarkXPress®, Adobe Illustrator®, Adobe Photoshop®, Adobe Streamline™, MacLink® *Plus*, Aldus® FreeHand™, Collage Plus™.

If you have comments or questions or would like to receive a free catalog, call or write:
Ziff-Davis Press
5903 Christie Avenue
Emeryville, CA 94608
800-688-0448

ISBN 1-56276-356-3

Manufactured in the United States of America

10 9 8 7 6 5 4 3 2 1

THANKS to my supportive and ever-so-svelte wife, Laura, who lent her opinions and saucy attitude to this project. Thanks honey.

And thanks to our kids, Jessie and Gabriel, who learned the hardship of "…Dad needs the Macintosh again…" Thanks kiddos. And to my mom who taught me that diligence is required in any endeavor worth doing.

Okay kids, you can have the Mac now.

THE INTERNET offers wonderfully instant, flexible, and cooperative communication, and that's how this book came to be.

I had been noticing the amusing personal signatures people appended to their e-mail postings. I went hunting for collections of these "sigs" and eventually discovered collectors who shared my fascination with the particular terse humor in them.

The collectors who passed along their quotes and humor are the foundation of this book. I spent many hours sorting out the submissions but I am indebted to those who shipped their collections to an uncertain fate. In a few cases, I was directed to retrieve a collection from an anonymous ftp site.

If you don't know what ftp is—well, don't worry about it. It's a way to get lots of information, just what you need more of.

Attributions

Each of the collectors supplied their best guesses on who actually wrote or spoke a quote. But attributions are tricky when items have been passed from person to person across numerous electronic highways. Inevitably some credits get dislodged or altered.

After I received a collection, if there was no attribution on a given item, I'd go hunting through the accumulated material to find a credit. And if that didn't work I'd go back out on the Net and request help. Even with all the suggestions offered, there are still items in this book that remain uncredited. My apologies to any person who created an item that lacks attribution.

Contribution

A percentage of any royalties realized from this book will be contributed to The Salvation Army.

What if You Also Collect Amusing Quotes?

I'd be very happy to hear from anyone with collections of humor like this book. You can e-mail me at the address below.

Merchandise

Some of the material in this book may be available on clothing or reprinted on cardboard cards suitable for display. For information send a note requesting details and listing your mailing address, both surface and e-mail, to:

Sunday
P.O. Box 847
Petaluma, CA 94953-0847

Our e-mail address for book projects is sunday@ix.netcom.com

THIS PROJECT has been a pleasant affirmation of cooperation. Thanks to the following contributors:

Mark Brader

Ken Breadner

Andrew Hamilton-Wright

Rich Holland

Heikki Karhunen

Jeff "Cruel to be Kind" Meyer, aka Moriarty

Craig Strickland

Thomas Strong

This Is
Your Brain
on the
Internet

Appropriate Technology

I'm all in favor of keeping dangerous weapons out of the hands of fools. Let's start with typewriters.

— **Solomon Short**

You can bring any calculator you like to the midterm, as long as it doesn't dim the lights when you turn it on.

— **Hepler, Systems Design 182**

If cars were designed the same way as software is today, they'd all have buggy-whip holders.

—**Marcus J. Ranum**

At This Rate of Growth...

"The NeXT (desktop computer): The hardware makes it a PC, the software makes it a Workstation, the unit sales make it a Mainframe."
NeXT was Steven Jobs' creation after founding Apple. The NeXTStep software was widely acclaimed, but the computers sold slowly.

The personal computer market is about the same size as the total potato chip market. Next year it will be about half the size of the pet food market and is fast approaching the total worldwide sales of pantyhose.

—**James Finke, president of Commodore Int'l Ltd., in 1982**

Comedy...& Its Opposing Force, Gravity

Real Americans Talk About Why They Chose the Sun SPARCstation 2000™:

"Last week we had a fella from Digital come out and look at the soybean crop. After 20 minutes, Ma chased him off and threw his keyboard out the window. We're from old Norwegian stock, and we know a thing or two about bus controllers."

—**Collected internally from a gag article at Sun Microsystems**

"Berkeley has two famous exports, Unix and LSD; this is not a coincidence."

My niece can't get enough of Hacker Barbie's Dream Basement Apartment! The pink Sun workstation in the corner, the little containers of takeout Szechuan scattered across the floor, her "Don't Blame Me, I voted Libertarian" T-shirt— it's on every little girl's Christmas list!

—**Kurt Hemr**

The Computing Culture

The architecture of the 80xxx series of microprocessors is clear evidence that Intel isn't doing in-house drug testing.

—**Paul Flaherty**

This is what separates us system programmers from the application programmers: We can ruin an entire machine and then recover it, they can only ruin their own files and then get someone else to restore them.

—**Geoff Collyer**

Calm down. It's only ones and zeros.

—**Sam Kass**

This one is an ANSI standard fuse blower.
**ANSI standards help establish conformance in the
computer field.**

—**Steven Hawthorne**

"Time Sharing: The use of many people by the
computer."

Never write device drivers while on acid!
**Device drivers are software written to control tools such
as printers.**

—**MJ Dominus**

Computing Road Signs

One item could not be deleted because it was
missing.

—**Macintosh System 7 error message**

"The world's coming to an end. Log off and leave
in an orderly fashion."

"Panic: No coffee found; programmer halted."

"A)bort R)etry I)nfluence with large hammer."

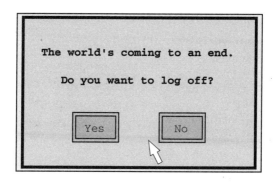

"Apathy Error: Don't bother striking any key."

"Bad command or file name. Go stand in the corner."

Demystifying Computer Programming

"Regression analysis: Mathematical techniques for trying to understand why things are getting worse."

"If you're smart enough to be a programmer, you're too smart to be a programmer."

"Programming is like sex: One mistake and you support it a lifetime."

If the standard says that (things) depend on the phase of the moon, the programmer should be prepared to look out the window as necessary.

—**Chris Torek**

There never has been, nor will there ever be, any programming language in which it is the least bit difficult to write bad code.

—**Lawrence Flon**

Discovered in the Workplace

If a train station is where the train stops, what's a work station?

—**Roger B. Dannenberg**

Automized and computerized industry requires more and more young men and women who have white-collar skills but behave with the docility expected of blue-collar workers.

—**Staughton Lynd,** *Newsweek,* **July 6, 1970**

Easily Forgotten

"Don't tell my mother I'm a programmer; she thinks I'm a piano player in a brothel."

The problem is between the chair and the keyboard.

—Jim T at NCR '91

Expectations

The only time the computers behave exactly as expected is when they're turned off.

—Daryl Crandall

The most likely way for the world to be destroyed, most experts agree, is by accident. That's where we come in; we're computer professionals. We cause accidents.

—**Nathaniel Borenstein**

I got a tab of BSD, man! It makes you see really cool networking things!
BSD is a version of Unix developed at U.C. Berkeley.
—**Tom Spindler**

The ultimate metric that I would like to propose for user friendliness is quite simple: If this system was a person, how long would it take before you punched it in the nose?

—**Tom Carey**

Fair Pricing

If the automobile had followed the same development cycles as the computer, a Rolls-Royce would today cost $100, get a million miles per gallon, and explode once a year.

—**Robert X. Cringely,** *InfoWorld*

Asked to look over the list of software purchased by the KGB, one American security expert concluded: "The Russians were rooked." The KGB paid several thousand dollars for a word processor, called GNU Emacs, which is widely distributed free in western universities.

—*The Economist*

Man is the best computer we can put aboard a spacecraft… and the only one that can be mass produced with unskilled labor.

—**Wernher von Braun**

Getting Started with Computers

"Daddy, what does 'FORMATTING DRIVE C' mean?"

"Trying to establish voice contact—please yell into keyboard."

"Keyboard: The keyboard is used for entering errors into a computer."

"Your password is
pitifully obvious."

The most overlooked advantage to owning a
computer is that if they foul up, there's no law
against whacking them around a little.

—Porterfield

"This is what happens when I roll my head on the
keyboard:
  kl,miojunhygbtmki,lo'/,kmoijunhybgtvfrcdnmk
il,o;p/ijn"

Hail Our Visionary Leaders

I think there's a world market for about five
computers.

> —**T.J. Watson of IBM in the 1940s**

Bill Gates says no matter how much more power
we can supply, he'll develop some really exciting
software that will bring the machine to its knees.

> —**Intel VP David House,** *EE Times,* **1989**

Illusions

Selling software is like prostitution; you've got it,
you sell it, you've still got it!

> —**D. Lambert**

Industrial Jokesters

An empty Saab Automobile factory in Sweden
got a little too mobile last month when a mispro-
grammed assembly line jump-started itself and
assembled 24 cars, rolling them off one after the
other into a wall. A worker finally discovered the

auto-automated line, but not before it had created
an impressive chrome-and-steel pileup. Saab offi-
cials said that damage was minimal: "Assembly
lines run slowly, and we have big bumpers," a
Saab spokesman said.

—*Newsweek,* June 7, 1993

NASA scientists finally contact the Mars Observer
space probe, only to be greeted by an answering
machine that does nothing except repeat, over
and over in a very pleasant voice: "Your call is
important to us."

—Dave Barry's "1993 in Review"

They just sent out announcements for the
conference on Massively Parallel systems. I got
600 of them.
**Massively parallel computers employ banks of processors
harnessed together.**

—Andy Koenig

**Excerpt from conversation between customer support
person and customer working for a well-known military-
affiliated research lab:**

    —You're not our only customer, you know.
    —But we're one of the few with tactical nuclear
    weapons.

Innovation

Where a calculator on the ENIAC is equipped
with 18,000 vacuum tubes and weighs 30 tons,
computers in the future may have only 1,000
vacuum tubes and weigh only 1½ tons.
                    —*Popular Mechanics,* **March 1949**

The proof that
IBM didn't
invent the car is
that it has a
steering wheel
and an accelerator
instead of spurs and
ropes, to be compatible
with a horse.
                    —**Jac Goudsmit**

Any company large enough to have a research lab
is large enough not to listen to it.
                    —**Alan Kay, computer futurist**

ARE YOU STILL GETTING YOUR NEWS
FROM DEAD TREES?

**—Headline in ad for *NewsPage*,
an electronic news medium**

Invention

There is no practical reason to create machine in-
telligences indistinguishable from human ones.
People are in plentiful supply. Should a shortage
arise, there are proven and popular methods for
making more. The point of using machines ought
to be they perform differently than people, and
preferably better.

—*The Economist*

No magnets were destroyed. This file was made
with 100 percent recycled magnetic media, com-
posed entirely of reclaimed, wasted disk space.

—Michael Regoli

It's a Test

If I ever hear of anyone compromising quality in order to make shipments, I will personally have them fired.

> —**David Packard, co-founder of Hewlett-Packard, 1977**

Beta Test: v. To voluntarily entrust one's data, one's livelihood and one's sanity to hardware or software intended to destroy all three. In earlier days, virgins were used to beta test volcanoes.

> —*The New Hackers' Dictionary,* **edited by Eric Raymond**

Crawling Horror: n. Ancient crusty hardware or software that is kept obstinately alive by forces beyond the control of the hackers at a site...the thing described is not just an irritation but an active menace to health and sanity. "mostly we code new stuff in C, but they pay us to maintain one big FORTRAN II application from nineteen-sixty-X that's a real crawling horror...."

> —*The New Hackers' Dictionary,* **edited by Eric Raymond**

Life on the Network

An MIT study predicts the median age of Internet users will drop from 26 to 15 within the next five years…and 85 percent of Internet users will not notice the difference.

—**Matt Crawford**

"Okay you workstations, start singing…'This LAN is your LAN, this LAN is my LAN…'"

There are three kinds of death in this world. There's heart death, there's brain death and there's being off the network.

—**Guy Almes**

Go not to Usenet for answers, for they will say both yes and no and "try another newsgroup."

—**Chris Croughton**

If addiction is judged by how long a dumb animal will sit pressing a lever to get a "fix" of something to its own detriment, then I would conclude that netnews is far more addictive than cocaine.

—**Robert Stampfli**

Common sense isn't any more common on
Usenet than it is anywhere else.

—**Henry Spencer**

That is one of the Laws of Usenet, up there with
"You can tell when a Usenet discussion is getting
old when someone drags out Hitler and the Nazis."

—**David Goldfarb**

E-mail isn't worth the paper it's printed on.

—**Brian T. Schellenberger**

Usenet: A place where you can be annoyed by
people you otherwise never would have met.

—**Nancy Lebovitz,** *The Button Lady*

I know this, because I encounter them on the
Internet, which is a giant international network
of intelligent, informed computer enthusiasts, by
which I mean, "people without lives." We don't
care. We have each other, on the Internet. "Geek
pride," that is our motto.

—**Dave Barry**

Selections from "Top Ten Reasons to Connect to The Internet"

  9. Feeling the need, the need for 45 Mbps speed.

  8. World Champion Wrestling is fake and you must let everyone know it.

  1. Occasional irregularity won't hinder you from getting good throughput.

—**Tracy LaQuey Parker**

Usenet is like Tetris for people who still remember how to read.

—**Joshua Heller**

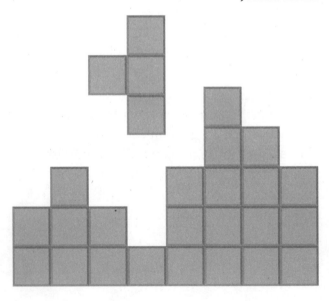

Living with the Animals

If you were plowing a field what would you rather use: two strong oxen or 1,024 chickens?

—Seymour Cray, Father of the Super Computer, talking about a design of computers based on parallel processing principles.

Science is not a sacred cow. Science is a horse. Don't worship it. Feed it.

—Aubrey Eben

Math: The Purest Science

—We're engineers.
 —What's Pi?
 —Oh, about three."

—Jen Quiren

"Prime number: Tender, juicy numbers used only in expensive computers."

"Base 8 is just like base 10, really—if you're missing two fingers."

Memories Are Made of This

Personally, my favorite sequence was the one about the crabs fighting each other for territory in the pool of liquefied bat guano where they spend their entire lives. In addition to being amusing, it was a wonderful metaphor for some aspects of my previous career in the computer industry.

—Joe Chew

Some people don't see the advantages of combining Microsoft applications. But then some people didn't see what would come of mixing nitro and glycerin.

—Recent Microsoft ad

The only thing obsoleted by Windows 3.1 is poking myself in the eye with a pointed stick.

—Gene Lee

Modern Titles

Systems Goddess
Describing Beth E. Binde, a Systems Programmer
—Dan Birchall

Systems Admiral
Describing Zaphod Khan

Predictions

The future, according to some scientists, will be
exactly like the past, only far more expensive.
—**John Sladek**

In ten years, computers will just be bumps in cables.
—**Gordon Bell, technologist**

There is no reason for any individual to have a
computer in their home.
—**Ken Olson, founder of Digital Equipment Co.**
speaking in 1977

Programming: The Wizard's Art

When your hammer is C++, everything begins to look like a thumb.
C++ is a popular object oriented programming language.
—Steve Haflich

For openers, the worst week of my life was spent learning C and programming an 8051 ($2 washing machine controller) to talk to an IBM PC. After ten years hacking Lisp Machines, God had finally sent me a machine commensurate with my abilities.
—Philip Greenspun

FORTRAN: Then, as now, the language used by scientists with real problems.
FORTRAN is the traditional first choice language of many scientists.
—Cambridge University Math Department

Professional stunt programmer. Do not attempt this at home.
—Vincent Needham

A Lisp programmer knows the value of everything, but the cost of nothing.
—Alan Perlis

When faced with a problem, some people say,
"Let's use AWK." Now they have two problems.
AWK is a Unix-based software utility.

> —Zalman Stern, former ITC hacker deity

"Programming is like pinball. The reward for
doing it is the opportunity to do it again."

Applicants must also have extensive knowledge of
Unix, although they should have sufficiently
good programming taste to not consider this an
achievement.

> —Ad in *The Boston Globe*

Quality Control

I have a spelling checker
It came with my PC
It plainly marks four my revue
Mistakes I cannot sea
I've run this poem threw it
I'm sure your pleased too no
Its letter perfect in it's weigh
My checker tolled me sew.

> —Pennye Harper

When the grammar checker identifies an error, it suggests a correction and can even makes some changes for you.

—*Microsoft Word for Windows 2.0 User's Guide,* p. 35

Real World Engineering

"A distributed system is one in which the failure of a computer you didn't even know existed can render your own computer unusable."

"Engineering is a lot like art: Some circuits are like lyric poems, some are like army manuals, and some are like *The Hitchhiker's Guide to the Galaxy.*"

Real World Science

The most exciting phrase to hear in science, the one that heralds new discoveries, is not "Eureka!" (I found it!) but "That's funny…."

—Isaac Asimov

Ludwig Boltzmann, who spent much of his life studying statistical mechanics, died in 1906, by his own hand. Paul Ehrenfest, carrying on the work, died similarly in 1933. Now it is our turn to study statistical mechanics.

—**David L. Goodman**

Realized Value

The less you know about home computers, the more you'll want the new IBM PS/1.

—**Ad in** *The Edmonton Journal*

Recognizing Credentials

—No. The dead cattle weren't only mutilated. They were burned by laser beams. Cows cannot turn a laser beam on their fellows.
—Laser beams? Are you SURE?
—I didn't get all this Pyrex with Green Stamps. I'm a scientist.

—*Man-Eating Cow*

Computer security is a missionary sell. You have
to convince them that there is a God, and that
you are a legitimate representative of that God.
> —**From the 2nd Computer Misuse and Anomaly
> Detection Workshop, U.C. Davis**

Religious Doctrine

"The program is absolutely right; therefore the
computer must be wrong."

Maybe Computer Science should be in the
College of Theology.
> —**R.S. Barton**

Revelations

"Hi. You have just entered the fourth dimension.
Small, isn't it?"

—Why do computers manage to do things so quickly?

—They don't have to answer the phone.

Romantic Wisdom

The woman of my dreams knows how to break into systems.

  —**Doug Tygar**

She thought she was going on a dream date…But soon, she'll live through every woman's nightmare: A DATE WITH AN ENGINEER!!
  —A skit from the Seattle-based "Almost Live" show

Simple Truths

What we call "Progress" is the exchange of one nuisance for another nuisance.
                              —Henry Havelock Ellis

Solutions On Parade

Limitless vistas of knowledge stretch before you. The touch of a key or the flick of a mouse may command entire domains of intellect. The cerebral pressings of countless harvests beg to slake your thirst for knowledge. You can look stuff up real easy.
                    —From the Willow network "Looker Upper"

"What this country needs is a good five-cent microcomputer."

"Meeting: An assembly of computer experts coming together to decide what person or department not represented in the room must solve the problem."

We're thinking about upgrading from SunOS 4.1.1 to SunOS 3.5.

—Henry Spencer

I've finally learned what "upward compatible" means. It means we get to keep all our old mistakes.

—Dennis van Tassel

Someone Somewhere Is Dying to Support Your Computer

A system admin's life is a sorry one. The only advantage he has over Emergency Room doctors is that malpractice suits are rare. On the other hand, ER doctors never have to deal with patients installing new versions of their own innards!

—Michael O'Brien

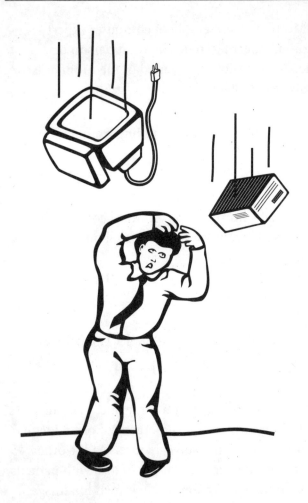

What goes up must come down. Ask any system administrator.

—Seen in a signoff line, but uncredited

This is one of those questions that reveals that I give computer support in the kingdom of the blind where having one eye and remembering to check if it's plugged in makes you the computer expert.

—**Mary Anne Salmon**

Speaking the Language

Computer Terms Defined:

Crash: Normal termination of a program.

Downtime: Slang for when a programmer is being realistic.

Execution: What your computer did to your program, also known as murder.

Hexadecimal: Unlucky numbers used by computers.

Mainframe: What the salesman said you were getting when you bought your micro.

Password: The nonsense word taped to your CRT.

Reset: Another way to end a four-hour sort.

When the machines are high-priced or when only a mathematician can understand them, we use the two-dollar word "automation;" when the machine is an average-priced one that high school students can understand, the one-dollar word "mechanization" is used; for low-priced machines any one can operate, we use the 50-cent word "labor-saving."

—**Donald & Eleanor Laird, *How to Get Along with Automation*, 1964**

The Pessimist's Guide to Engineer-Talk:
—What they say: "We've noticed some failure evidence."
—What they mean: "Something's burning."
—**From rec.humor.funny**

Instead of saying "All computer systems will be bar-coded" for inventory purposes, a document was published stating "all computer systems will be barricaded."

—**Jim Vecht**

It talks to me in gibberish like "ProComm," a term that is unnerving to a survivor of the McCarthy era.
—**Mary McGrory in** *The Washington Post*

Still a Great Entertainer!

Selections From Eclectic Music Survey # 5:
Todd Rundgren:
As good a Macintosh programmer as he is
a musician.

—**Cliff Tuel**

Succeeding

Software suppliers are trying to make their software packages more "user-friendly." Their best
approach, so far, has been to take all the old
brochures and stamp the words, "user-friendly"
on the cover.

—**Bill Gates**

Surprising Industrial Facts

Imagine if every Thursday your shoes exploded if
you tied them the usual way. This happens to us all
the time with computers, and nobody thinks of
complaining.

—**Jeff Raskin in *Dr. Dobb's Journal***

I can direct dial, today, a man my parents warred with. They wanted to kill him, I want to sell software to him.

—**Brad Templeton**

Technical work needs reviewing for the same reason that pencils need erasers.

—**Freedman & Weinberg**

If we don't provide support to our users, someone is bound to confuse us with Microsoft.

—**Charles "Chip" Yamasaki**

Technology in Perspective

And, of course, you have the commercials where savvy business people get ahead by using their Macintosh computers to create the ultimate American business product: a really sharp-looking report.

—**Dave Barry**

It would take 100 clerks working for 100 years to make a mistake as monumental as a single computer can make in one thousandth of a second.

—*Dental Economics*, November, 1968

Technology Truisms

Any sufficiently advanced technology is indistinguishable from Magic.

—**Arthur C. Clarke**

Terminology

Computer terms glossary:

Computer Geek: n. One who eats (computer) bugs for a living. One who fulfills the dreariest negative stereotypes about hackers: an asocial, malodorous, pasty-faced monomaniac with all the personality of a cheese grater.

—*The New Hacker's Dictionary,* **edited by Eric Raymond**

Drool-proof Paper: n. Documentation that has been obsessively dumbed down, to the point where only a cretin could bear to read it, is said to have succumbed to the "drool-proof paper syndrome." (Such as) "Do not expose your LaserWriter to open fire or flame."

—*The New Hacker's Dictionary,* **edited by Eric Raymond**

Loop: See Infinite Loop…Infinite Loop: See Loop

Manual: A unit of documentation. There are always three or more of a given item. One is on the shelf; someone has the others. The information you need is in the others.

Crash: A sudden, unexpected cessation of activity by the computer, accompanied by a sudden, unexpected increase in activity by the system administrator. Caused by someone running their huge, unimportant program just as your small, critical program is about to finish.

—Ray Simard (Alan Silverstein)

"**Tremendous Expandability:** The unbundled 'bare-bones' system with the low advertised price is virtually useless."

"**Compatible with Most Systems:** Favor us with a big enough order and we'll start designing an interface."

To Laugh at Men of Sense Is the Privilege of Fools

Inventions reached their limit long ago, and I see no hope for further development.

—**Julius Frontinus, First Century** A.D.

Touring the Universe

```
              You are here       (Our solar system)
  \~              |
  |~      .    o    o    .   :;:  ( )  -o-   o  . o
  |~
  /~
```

—**Craig Levin**

Truths of Leadership

Announced today was a new operating system for the PC. It is called "DOS/Perot." When you boot it, it displays a message on the screen saying it's thinking of running. It then scans the hard drive, looking for competing OSs. If any competing OSs are found, it quits immediately.

—**Robert X. Cringely**

At Group L, Stoffel oversees six first-rate programmers—a managerial challenge roughly comparable to herding cats.

—*The Washington Post Magazine*

Unavoidable Truths of Computing

"Computers are like Old Testament Gods: Lots of rules and no mercy."

This is just the result of someone sitting down before a computer and carefully removing his head first.

—**Leonard Wibberley**

"And remember—every time you link up to a computer, you are linking up to every computer that computer has ever linked up to."

"Applications programming is a race between software engineers who strive to produce idiot-proof programs, and the Universe which strives to produce bigger idiots."

"When solving a panic you must first ask yourself what were you doing that could possibly frighten an operating system."

Unix: The Culture Masquerading As an Operating System

Unix is the answer, but only if you phrase the question very carefully.

—**Kurt J. Lidl**

"Manual? What manual?!? This is Unix, my son, you just gotta *know*!!!"

"Unix (the operating system) is like the maritime transit system in an impoverished country. The ferryboats are dangerous as Hell, offer no protection from the weather and leak like sieves. Every monsoon season a couple of them capsize and drown all the passengers but people still line up for them and crowd aboard."

Up on the Big Screen

If some unemployed punk in Trenton, New Jersey, lying on a sofa with a bong can get a cassette to make love to Elle McPherson for $19.95, this virtual reality stuff is going to make crack look like Sanka.

—**Dennis Miller**

Things I'd Like To See, #241: A Web page for the *Weekly World News.* The thought of being able to click here and see a 450K MPEG of a two-headed cow giving birth to Satan fills me with unspeakable glee.

—**crisper@armory.com**

We're kind of like an information superhighway without the information.

—**David Letterman**

—How do you tell if a moron has been using your terminal?
—There is white-out on the monitor.

Usenet

Usenet is like a herd of performing elephants with diarrhea—massive, difficult to redirect, awe-inspiring, entertaining, and a source of mind-boggling amounts of excrement when you least expect it.

—**Gene Spafford**

Come to think of it, there are already a million monkeys on a million typewriters, and Usenet is nothing like Shakespeare.

—Blair Houghton

Spelling on Usenet is like dancing at the Republican National Convention: badly executed, occasionally funny to watch, but for the most part completely ignored.

—Christian Wagner

Virtually Hollywood

—What is the difference between *Jurassic Park* and IBM?
—One is a high-tech theme park filled with dinosaurs, and the other is a Steven Spielberg movie.

—Jan Falcona (modified by Jeff Meyer)

Who They Really Are

My father peddles opium,
    My mother's on the dole.
My sister used to walk the streets
    But now she's on parole.
My uncle plays with little girls,
    My aunt, she raped a steer,
But they won't even speak to me
    'cause I'm an engineer
        —The MIT Engineers' Drinking Song